This book is dedicated to Jay Lose and Charles Lose.

Text by Anne Swartz

ISBN: 978-1-960852-13-7 (Paperback)
ISBN: 978-1-960852-14-4 (eBook)

Published by Aram Samsam Printing

The image on the cover is Hiroshige II (Ichiusai Shigenobu) (1826-69)/Japanese, A White Cat Playing with a String, 1863, colour woodblock print, Minneapolis Institute of Arts, 8 3/8 x 10 1/2 in. (21.3 x 26.7 cm) © Minneapolis Institute of Art / Bequest of Richard P. Gale / Bridgeman Images.

Once upon a time, there was a happy white cat named Snowball. Snowball lived in a beautiful house with a kind lady named Maya. They loved each other very much.

Snowball liked to curl up outside and relax, watching the world.

Snowball loved simple toys in his house. While playing with his toys one day, he glimpsed something blue move past the window.

On this exciting day, Snowball ran outside through the busy streets of his Tokyo neighborhood. "Wee, this is fun!" Snowball thought.

Soon, he spotted a blue string dancing in the wind. It twirled and whirled like a dragon at a big party. "Wow, what a fun toy!" Snowball thought and decided to follow it.

Snowball felt brave. "I'm a strong ninja cat," he thought, puffing up his fluffy chest. With the blue string in sight, he was ready for a big adventure!

Snowball's eyes locked on the tantalizing string, which seemed to evade him playfully.

The blue string led Snowball on a chase around the city.

The string wound around, gliding between other cats.

Some cats on the street seemed excited about the blue string and chased after it for a little while.

The street got steep, and the other cats got tired. Snowball kept climbing and continued following the blue string.

At the top of a hill, Snowball looked down on the city and saw the blue string continuing to circle. Snowball jumped down and ran on after the string.

With a brave "Meow!" he continued the chase.

Stripes and Patches had been enjoying the day inside, cozily relaxing. Snowball's loud meowing outside woke them up.

They went outside. A playful twinkle appeared in their eyes, matching the one in Snowball's eyes. But before they could start chasing the string, they smelled some fish and went off to find food.

Snowball remained focused on the chase. "Can you catch me, Snowball?" the string seemed to tease. And he continued after it.

Snowball didn't stop. He kept running and leaping.

With a triumphant meow and a final energetic leap, he finally caught the blue string!

"Hooray! I caught you!" he thought, feeling like the bravest cat in Tokyo!

He always enjoyed the beautiful outdoors and appreciated the lovely countryside. Finding the blue string had been a special treat.

After the great adventure, Snowball walked home, feeling very happy.

The blue string, his new friend, was as tired as he was, but they were both content.

Back at home, Snowball curled up for a good, long nap.

He dreamed about strings of all colors and fun chases. As he fell asleep, he thought, "Today was fun!"

Snowball was a brave white cat. He knew the next day would bring a new game to his happy life.

Excited, he fell asleep, dreaming of adventures.

Snowball woke up to a new day full of possibilities. Going out and finding the blue string had been a BIG change. Would this new day include more string chases?

There would be more places to explore in his beloved Tokyo neighborhood. Capturing the blue string had been a big prize for Snowball.

Each purr from Snowball was a sign of his happiness. Every flick of his tail showed his bravery.

www.ingramcontent.com/pod-product-compliance
Lightning Source LLC
LaVergne TN
LVHW052302100826
845147LV00001B/122

* 9 7 8 1 9 6 0 8 5 2 1 3 7 *